I0418675

Wandering Woman: Utah

The Ultimate Road Trip: One Woman's
Journey Across the United States by Car

Julie Bettendorf

Copyright © [2022] by [Julie Bettendorf]

All rights reserved.

No portion of this book may be reproduced in any form without written permission from the publisher or author, except as permitted by U.S. copyright law.

Contents

Introduction

"Not all who wander are lost."

Are you sure? I thought to myself, as I tried not to panic. I was a long way from anything familiar, but that was how it should be. I had driven thousands of miles on dusty, pothole-filled roads. It's often on the worst roads that you can discover something truly amazing.

My dusty CRV was parked beside me, containing one restless dog and a variety of snack bags, all empty by now. There were no buildings in sight, no cars or people or movement at all. Only the constant humming of the insects as they buzzed around my head.

I turned to my left – another straight road that trailed off into the distance. I glanced over to the right, then behind me – two more barely discernible roads stretched out into the abyss. I was in a four-way intersection with no signs, no sense of direction, and no sign of life for several miles. No cell service either, and that meant no GPS. *Damn*, I thought. *I'm lost.*

How did I get here? I couldn't help but feel like this little intersection was a cruel metaphor for life. I began to daydream, imagining each road might transport me back to a different time, a different role in my life, and a different me.

If I took the road from whence I came, it could lead me all the way back to Oregon, back to my cheating third husband, back to a life of loneliness and solitude. There is no greater loneliness than being married to someone who isn't actually present in your life.

If I took the road to my left, perhaps it could take me back to my career as a dental hygienist, a job I hated deep down in my soul. There is something so disengaging about cleaning teeth for a living. It's a disgusting, smelly way to get a paycheck. It pays well, which is great, but the best part is the huge gob of friends I enjoy to this day.

Or maybe the road to my right, *yes – maybe that's the path*, I imagined. Maybe it could take me back to my real treasure, my kids. Back to their smiling, innocent faces as toddlers, as they danced around the Christmas tree and their father and I were still married. Back when they still needed me for every little thing.

But, that was just it. I didn't feel needed anymore. My kids weren't toddlers anymore – they were both full-grown adults, and far too busy for me. My dental buddies were still working, but I wasn't. Dental hygiene had robbed me of the cartilage in my fingers, giving me severe, disabling arthritis. And, I wouldn't be returning to any more husbands either, because three marriages were quite enough for me.

All three of these paths, all three of these roles – the wife, the mother, and the dental hygienist – had seemingly been stripped from me within a year. I was lost and looking to find myself again.

The funny thing about this phrase, "not all who wander are lost"– is that, in my experience, wandering and being lost walk hand-in-hand with one another, and the expression can be flipped. In my experience, not all who are lost are wandering, and that is a real disservice to the beauty and clarity that the world has to offer.

When one becomes lost, wandering is the only option to guide oneself back to a path. After all, one could not come upon any dirt path at all without wandering.

—❖—

I began wandering at an early age, both with my mind and with my feet. At eight years old, I was reading a book about archaeology and dreaming of one day seeing Egypt. I didn't follow a traditional path in high school either, going heavily into foreign languages, in hopes of one day using them.

At twenty-five years old, I divorced my first husband (the dental student who talked me into becoming a dental hygienist so I could work for him) and decided to give traveling a real shot. I took off for the Andes and Macchu Picchu, climbing up ancient Inca stone steps to reach the magnificent ruins.

Anyone who has been to Macchu Picchu will tell you there is something ethereal and deeply spiritual about the place. The ruins stretch out across the emerald green mountains, way up in the middle of the sky. Macchu Picchu gave me my first experience of feeling history. This trip inspired me to come back and complete a degree in archaeology, and I've been wandering ever since.

More travel followed including a backpack trip around Europe for three months, by myself, and trips to Britain, Italy, and Greece. I visited the burial places of Crusaders, mummies, and ancient kings. I happened upon the castle of my namesake in Bettendorf, Luxembourg, and wandered my way through European history.

My favorite excursion by far was finally seeing Egypt with my daughter in 2012. Just like my childhood dream envisioned, I rode a camel beneath the pyramids of Giza, with my head wrapped in some man's sweaty turban. It was perfect.

Traveling has always been my own personal antidote to pain. I went to Mexico after my first and second divorces, Canada after my third, and Italy after my dad died. Call it avoidance if you want, but I call it an accelerated form of healing in the purest sense of the word. I believe travel can heal your soul.

Wandering has always worked its wonders on me – made me feel renewed, rejoiceful, grateful, and purposeful. It's been my medicine.

So, as I stood in that intersection, I once again wondered how wandering had led me so astray this time. *What the hell am I supposed to do now?* It was then that I realized that one last path had not been considered yet – the path which stretched straight out in front of me. *Which role does this represent?* I pondered.

The answer smacked me in the face.

That last dirt road – the only path that could take me where I wanted to go, the only path that ever truly healed me or showed me the way – was the path of the traveler. The wife, the mother, and the hygienist roles – though valued in their time – were sitting in the bleachers now. It was time to welcome and enable my boldest, bravest, and perhaps most pivotal role yet:

The role of the Wandering Woman.

Welcome to Wandering Woman

This book is for you – the grieving empty nester mom, the begrudged housewife, the woman in need of a drastic change in her life. Really, this book is for anyone with a passion for traveling. If you feel lost with no sense of direction or purpose in life, that's a bonus – this book will be even more appealing to you. And lastly, if you're a man reading this book, congratulations for holding a book with the word woman in the title. You're contributing to gender equality, and that's pretty neat.

I decided to combine three of my dearest loves – travel, history, and archaeology – and put them into a book because I believe wandering has the power to change your life. I have been to many areas of the world and had too many outstanding experiences to list. However, by the time both my children had moved out in 2017, I had never seen my own country – America.

Me

It was the perfect time to explore
a new country (my own) and discover a new me at the same time.

So, I packed up my Honda CRV, along with some gear and my 14-year-old furry friend, Sadie. ***Wandering Woman*** is the chronicle of my journey across eleven states, discovering the joy of getting lost and finding myself along the way

Why America?

A merica, the beautiful? I sure think so, but I didn't realize just how beautiful our country is until I embarked on traveling across eleven western states in a year.

The United States offers everything for the discerning palate. From spectacular beaches, austere mountains, to rolling plains, our country has it all. It's difficult to comprehend just how large and impressive our scenery is, until you experience it first-hand, with the ultimate road trip.

I also realized just how much of our history is missing from U.S. history I was taught as a kid. The history of our country didn't begin with the pilgrims landing on Plymouth Rock in the 1600s. Our history is far more ancient, with rock art and archaeological sites dating back over 12,000 years.

We also owe a tremendous debt to early pioneers who tamed our land. The Mormons and other groups ventured into the great unknown with their families and their worldly possessions. Some of them pulled cumbersome handcarts across the country to settle in inhospitable, dangerous locations.

The goal of **Wandering Woman** is to bring history back to life and make it interesting again. I am presenting some famous sites, and many little-known ones. You will take the road-less-traveled with me, while we explore ghost towns, rock art sites, archaeological sites, and museums, to discover the colorful tapestry that is our country.

I present some history, including dates, but my goal is to present more of the real-life stories of history, including ghost stories, profiles in history, voices from the past, and moments in time, to give you, the reader, a deeper understanding of the context of history.

This is by no means an exhaustive list of places to visit. In fact, I encourage you to discover America for yourself, as I did, by making a trek across the land by car. You can explore as the early explorers did, just a little more comfortably, with a lot less hardship.

I hope you enjoy this book and take a little time out to discover our beautiful country, and maybe even discover yourself in the process.

Safe Travels,

Julie Bettendorf

Welcome to Utah

The Beehive State

*U**tah*** is a paradise for the outdoor person. Its magnificent rock formations and spectacular national monuments provide countless exploring opportunities. Utah has a rich history to enjoy with early rock art sites to early Mormon settlements to abandoned towns. Utah beckons you to come visit and stay awhile.

5 things to love about Utah:

The spectacular, stark beauty of the numerous rock formations

The inspiring national monuments like Hovenweep and Natural Bridges

The awe-inspiring dinosaur sites like Mule Canyon

The many rock art sites like Sego Canyon and Nine Mile Canyon

The early Mormon pioneering history from places like Grafton and Capitol Reef

Dreams of Utah

"*As we crossed the Colorado-Utah border I saw God in the sky in the form of huge gold sunburning clouds above the desert that seemed to point a finger at me and say, "Pass here and go on, you're on the road to heaven."* – **Jack Kerouac**

"*Stepping out onto any lookout, you are invited to connect with an amazing example of some of the most unusual terrain on this planet, making you feel as though you are stepping foot on the edge of another world.*" – **Stefanie Payne**

"*It would honestly not have surprised me to see Butch Cassidy and the Sundance Kid plunging from an unforgiving precipice into the river below.*" – **Karl Wiggins**

Early Utah

Fielding Garr Ranch 1930s
(courtesy of Fielding Garr Ranch)

Freighting Along Nine Mile Road 1883

Early Park City, Utah
(courtesy Park City Museum)

Top Stuff to See in Utah

Favorite Utah Rock Art Sites:

- Sego Canyon
- Nine Mile Canyon

Favorite Utah Historical Sites:

- Simpson Springs Pony Express Station
- Capitol Reef National Monument

Favorite Utah Archeological Sites:

- Hovenweep National Monument
- Fremont Indian State Park

Favorite Utah Museums:

- Edge of the Cedars Museum

- Park City Museum

When driving through Utah, be on the lookout for:

E xquisite scenery and wild horses

Northern Utah

Simpson Springs Pony Express Station

Ogden

Downtown Ogden

O *gden*, named for explorer Peter Skene Ogden, has a wonderful *25ᵗʰ* *Street* which contains a number of beautiful historic buildings turned into shops and restaurants. The street is anchored by the **Union Station** at the far end.

Ogden has some eclectically **painted horse statues** all over town. They are quite spectacular, each one different from the rest.

When you are in Ogden, don't miss **Peery's Egyptian Theatre**. The theatre was built by the brothers Harman and Louis Peery, descendants of a pioneer businessman, David H. Peery in 1923.

The theatre was to be "The Showplace of the West." The theatre opened on July 3, 1924 and contained 1200 seats. The theatre has a day to night sky, complete with twinkling stars. It is now a venue for the world-famous Sundance Film Festival.

Peery's Egyptian Theatre

How to get to Ogden:

Ogden is located 35 miles north of Salt Lake City, on I-15.

Salt Lake City

Antelope Island Bison

To get to magnificent **Antelope Island** park in the middle of the Great Salt Lake, you travel across a causeway. The island is over 28,000 acres of beauty, with long, golden fields, and stark rock outcroppings. The real stars are the herds of wildlife, especially bison. The hundreds of bison are descendants of the original twelve animals brought to the island in 1893.

Antelope Island was first inhabited over 6,000 years ago, but the first modern settlers came in 1848, establishing the *Fielding Garr Ranch*.

The ranch is an interesting place to visit, and you should begin your visit with a stop at the *Orientation Center*, which has numerous artifacts of early ranching life.

On the grounds of the ranch, you can visit many buildings including a *sheep wagon*, providing a fascinating look into how a shepherd lived. There were 10,000 sheep on Antelope Island. Mormon founder Brigham Young was one of many to keep his livestock on the island.

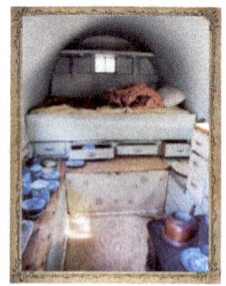

The ***ranch house*** has a living room built in 1848, and a kitchen added on in the 1880s.

Another interesting building is the ***spring house***, the first refrigeration room on Antelope Island. _{Utah State Parks}

How to get to Antelope Island:

Antelope Island State Park is north of Salt Lake City. Travel north on I-15, take exit 332 and drive west for 15 miles. You come upon the causeway to enter the park. There is an entrance fee of $10 per car.

Simpson Springs

Simpson Springs Pony Express Station

Simpson **Springs Pony Express Station** is part of the **Onaqui Wild Horse Management Area**.

The spring was discovered by Captain Simpson of the US Army in 1858. This station became an important source of water and horses for the Pony Express starting in 1860. Corbett

When you are checking out the Pony Express Station, don't forget to look for the beautiful wild horses at Onaqui. There are spectacular wild horses all over the place!

They are the descendants of horses brought here by European settlers in the late 1800s. The Onaqui Wild Horse Management Area has 206,878 acres for the horses to run wild. Utah State Parks

How to get to Simpson Springs Pony Express Station:

The Simpson Springs Pony Express Station is located near the town of Tooele. Drive south on Hwy 36 to the Pony Express turnoff.

A word about Pony Express history:

Before horses were used to carry mail, a mail carrying system known as "jackass mail" was tried out. George Chorpenning and Absolom Woodward contracted with the federal government to use mules to haul the mail. Jackass mail was short-lived, and its founders were as well. Woodward was killed by Indians, and Chorpenning died penniless.

Camels were tried out too. Jefferson Davis, secretary of war came up with the idea in 1853. It was a big hit with Bible readers, but the camels didn't like the rocky terrain. Leather boots were made to protect their feet, but the camels were a failure. Some were sold as circus animals, and others were simply let loose in the desert. Corbett

Voices from the past:

"Wanted, young, skinny, wiry fellows not over eighteen. Must be expert riders, willing to risk death daily. Orphans preferred. Wages $25 a week" **job posting from a San Francisco newspaper, March 1860.** Corbett

"Greatest of all inventions to me, because it affected me directly, is the telegraph. In the two minutes we used to be allowed to change horses at a station, Western Union now sends a message to New York or even London. The telegraph today does in a second what it took eighty young men and hundreds of horses eight days to do when I was a rider in the Pony Express."
William Campbell, pony express rider, at age 94. Corbett

Fun facts about the Pony Express:

- The Pony Express ran from 1860 to 1861 and was replaced by the telegraph.

- The route ran from St. Joseph, Missouri to Sacramento, California, a distance of 1900 miles

- Highway 50, known as the "loneliest road in America" was part of the mail route from Sacramento to Salt Lake City in 1851.

- There were 190 stations along the route, when the Pony Express was in peak operation.

- Each station was equipped with 2 agents, 1 station keeper, and 1 assistant.

- There were 420 horses used at peak times, along with 80 riders.

- Pony Express riders weighed an average of 100 to 120 pounds, and their average age was 19.

- Horses were usually half-wild mustangs, famous for their speed and the fact that they never got tired.

- They rode an average speed of 7 miles per hour, which meant that it took them an average of 10 days to complete the trip.

- Each rider rode 60 to 120 miles before changing riders.

- The fastest ride ever was 7.5 days to deliver Abraham Lincoln's Inaugural address.

- William C. "Buffalo Bill" Cody rode 322 miles in 21 hours and 40 minutes using 21 horses.

- Riders were paid $120 to $125 per month.

- A letter cost $5 in gold, paid in advance. Corbett

Park City

Downtown Park City

***P**ark City* is a charming, historic mining town spreading down
the hillside. Silver was discovered here in 1868. After the

silver boom was over, the town reinvented itself as a world-class ski resort, hosting the Winter Olympics in 2002.

As you walk along the streets of Park City, one of the buildings that stands out is the ***Miner's Hospital***, built in 1904, which now houses the public library.

Be sure and pay a visit to the ***Park City Museum***, which contains an excellent sampling of historical photographs and mining lore. Don't forget to see the fascinating ***territorial jail.***

How to get to Park City, Utah:

Park City is located 35 miles from Salt Lake City off I-80.

Ghost story:

There is a legend about ***Tommyknockers*** that are said to haunt many mining camps. Tommyknockers got their name from Cornish miners who believed that little men lived underground and caused the knocking with their tiny hammers.

Some early miners believed Tommyknockers were good spirits who were warning of an impending mine collapse. Others believed that the person who heard the knocking would die. Still others believed that Tommyknockers were the spirits of miners who had died during a cave-in. Some miners even left offerings of food and drink to appease the Tommyknockers.

A word about mining terms:

Some common terms thrown about in the world of mining include:

- Prospecting-looking for material to be mined, usually in the form of a gold or silver vein trapped within quartz. This is known as "blossom rock."

- Placer mining-to find superficial deposits of gold in streams and rivers

- Lode mining-to find deposits of precious metals enclosed in rock

Miners in Leadville, CO
(courtesy of the town of Leadville)

Miners worked in extremely hazardous conditions, and the danger of their jobs may have led them to become highly superstitious. These are just a few of the superstitions miners believed in:

- Women were bad luck in the mines, especially if the woman was a redhead. It meant someone would die.

- Someone would also die if a black cat or a dog entered the mine.

- Whistling in a mine drove away good spirits and invited bad ones. Whistling was also believed to cause vibrations in the earth, prompting a cave-in.

- A cave-in was most likely to happen between midnight and 4 AM.

- Miners would often quit a day early because they believed they would be injured or killed on their last shift.

Park City Museum

Northeastern Utah

Dinosaur National Monument

Dinosaur National Monument

Dinosaur National Monument

T he ***Dinosaur National Monument*** goes through the border between Utah and Colorado. It's yet another destination with something for everyone from dinosaur fossils, to petroglyphs, homestead cabins, to beautiful scenery.

The ***Quarry Exhibit*** at the ***Visitor's Center*** has over 1500 Jurassic Era fossils that are over 149 million years old embedded in the rock wall. It's a sight to see.

There is also a rock shelter, nicknamed the ***"Swelter Shelter"*** by the archaeologists who excavated it. It was so named because of how hot it was during the summer, and these same archaeologists came down with an infection from the spores in the soil. The earliest occupation of the shelter dates to between 9000 and 6000 years ago. [Noble]

Within the shelter are numerous petroglyphs made by the Fremont culture.

The *Cub Creek Trail* within the park has an area of petroglyphs made by the Fremont people, including a 6-foot lizard that is at least 1000 years old, etched high up on a cliff face. This lizard is one of my favorite rock art images I've ever seen. The scale of it is magnificent.

Further along the Cub Creek Trail is the *Josie Morris homestead cabin* established by Josie Morris in the early 1900s.

She lived alone in the cabin for over 49 years, growing crops and raising cattle.

Dinosaur National Monument also has the beautiful **Green River Campground** on site.

How to get to Dinosaur National Monument, Utah:

Dinosaur National Monument is close to the city of Vernal in northeastern Utah. From Vernal, take Hwy 40 east for 12 miles to Jensen, then drive north on Hwy 149 for 7 miles to the entrance.

Profiles in history:

Josie Bassett (Morris) was married a total of 5 times, and was reputed to have had many lovers. She also had a crush on Butch Cassidy at one time, when Butch worked on the family's ranch.

She lived in her little cabin at Cub Creek, selling bootleg whiskey and apricot brandy. She also rustled cattle from nearby ranchers and was caught and went to trial in 1911. She was acquitted after stating "I'm a grandma, do I look like a cattle thief?"

Josie died in 1964 at 90 years old after breaking her hip. She lived an extraordinary life of walking the Overland Trail as a pioneer, surviving Indian attacks, and meeting famous outlaws, as well as being somewhat of an outlaw herself.

Voices from the past:

" I thought he was the most dashing and handsome man I ever seen. I was such a young thing...and looked upon Butch as my knight in shining armor. He was more interested in his horse than he was in me, and I remember being very put off by that. I went home after being snubbed by him and stamped my foot in frustration. " **Josie Bassett, on meeting Butch Cassidy when she was 15 years old.** Rutter

Central Utah

Nine Mile Canyon

Helper

Downtown Helper

Delightful **Helper** was originally settled in 1881, by Teancum Pratt and his multiple wives. Pratt ended up selling some of his property to the railroad, which came through in 1887.

The town got its name from the many extra engines it took to push a train up the steep grade known as soldier summit. These extra engines were known as "helpers."

It became a major junction of two railroads in 1892. The town grew because of extensive coal mining and railroad employment. Today, as you walk along the main street of Helper, you will feel transported back into Main Street America of the 1950s.

How to get to Helper, Utah:

Helper is about 110 miles southeast of Salt Lake City, and 7 miles northwest of Price.

Cleveland Lloyd Dinosaur Quarry

Cleveland Lloyd Dinosaur Quarry

T he ***Cleveland Lloyd Dinosaur Quarry*** is an arid, desolate place which has yielded up a treasure trove of dinosaur remains.

Earl Douglass found the first dinosaur bones from the quarry in August, 1909.

Since then, the bones of over 500 dinosaurs have come out of the quarry, including a dinosaur egg.

The quarry contains the most concentrated group of dinosaur bones from the Jurassic period in the world.

Cleveland Lloyd is named for Cleveland, which is the town closest to the site, and Malcolm Lloyd, the financier of the site.

How to get to Cleveland Lloyd Dinosaur Quarry:

The turnoff to the quarry is 12 miles south of Price, UT, off hwy. 10. You travel a gravel road for about 13 miles before coming to the quarry.

Nine Mile Canyon

Nine Mile Canyon

*N*ine Mile Canyon is a spectacular place, both for the scenery, and the wealth of rock art to be found there.

This is one of my favorite sites because of the number of images, and the superb condition they are in. The amazing petroglyphs are in the Fremont Style and date from 900 AD to 1300 AD. ^{Noble}

You will also see some historical graffiti carved by early pioneers. It too, is making its way into the archaeological record here, for you to enjoy.

The most famous images consist of a large hunting scene, known as the "Great Hunt" located at milepost 45.9. It is truly wonderful, with plentiful bighorn sheep, hunters with bows and arrows, and a large shamanistic figure with horns in the center top.

The detail and artistry in this petroglyph panel is remarkable. Carving these amazing figures using stone tools must have been arduous. The photos don't do justice to the spiritual beauty of the panel.

Take your time as you drive the meandering, paved road, and be on the lookout for small road signs. Many of the sites are well-marked with pull-outs for parking. One of the sites lies at the intersection of Nine Mile Canyon Road and Harmony Road.

Another beautiful site that offers a nice little hike is the Big Daddy Complex, located at the milepost 43.8. It has a large parking area and the hike is easy. Along with numerous images, there are also pictographs painted in a cave. The large images of elk are particularly impressive.

There is also a wonderful picnic area with an old homestead cabin, adding much to the ambience of Nine Mile Canyon. If I were a rancher, this is where I would want to be.

How to get to Nine Mile Canyon, Utah:

The beginning of the route is 7 miles south of Price off of Hwy 6/191. Turn left onto Soldier's Creek Road. Sites lay along this road for the next 45 miles.

A word about petroglyphs and pictographs:

Petroglyphs were made by taking river rock and heating it and then cooling it suddenly so it cracks to form a sharp tool. This tool was used to chisel along with another stone for a hammer to peck or incise the designs on rock. A thick desert coating called a patina was removed to expose the lighter rock underneath.

A **petroglyph panel** is a group of petroglyphs that tell a story. The Hopi describe the purpose of petroglyphs like this:

The Creator told the Hopi to make their mark on the land saying, "We were here." They built homes with rock, painted pottery and broke it into pieces when they left the land, and they put markings on walls so they could remember an area during migration. Indigenous people view petroglyphs as history, part of their culture, a culture that is ongoing. Chino

Pictographs, are painted instead of incised. They are drawn pictures using minerals like hematite mixed with a binder such as animal fat, urine, or oil to make paint.

The spiral sun symbol commonly represented may show Hopi migration, where they come from and where they have been. The images talk to the current Hopi people about their past history.

Pictograph colors are:

- Black, which is made with yellow ochre, pinon gum, and sumac

- Red, which is made with red ochre and mahogany root

- Yellow, which is made with rabbitbrush

- Plant oils and animal fats were used as binders

Buckhorn Wash

Buckhorn Wash

To get to **Buckhorn Wash**, you drive down a magnificent canyon on an unpaved, but passable road.

The first stop is a trail leading up to a group of petroglyphs, made by the Fremont culture about 1000 years ago. There are many images of bighorn sheep and other animals.

Next you reach Buckhorn Wash, with a large grouping over 100 feet long, of spirit figures with no legs. These spectacular figures are the work of the Archaic Barrier Canyon Culture from least 2000 years ago.

They are said to represent the Shaman's visions of death and transformation into a spirit. Birds, dogs and other animals were spiritual helpers to guide the healer to the sky or the underworld. Noble

How to get to Buckhorn Wash, Utah:

Buckhorn wash is near Green River. From Green River take I-70 west for 30 miles. Take exit 129 and drive 27 miles north to a gravel road which leads to the site.

A word about Barrier Canyon Style rock art:

Barrier Canyon Style got its name from a rock art site along Barrier Creek, in Canyonlands National Park. The style can be found in rock art sites of southeastern Utah, western Colorado, and northern Arizona.

A common theme in Barrier Canyon Culture rock art features anthropomorphic (human-like) figures without arms or legs. The figures typically have broad shoulders, tapered bodies, and bulging eyes. Dots, rays, and crowns can often be seen above the heads of the figures. They can be accompanied by dogs, birds, snakes, and other creatures. ^{Noble}

Eastern Utah

Sego Canyon

Sego Canyon

Sego Canyon

M agnificent *Sego Canyon* is unique because it contains 3 rock art styles, the Archaic, Fremont, and the Ute.

Archaic figures have no legs and seem to be floating in space.

The Fremont figures also have no legs. They have triangular bodies and large, elaborate necklaces. Bighorn sheep are common in Fremont art.

Both Archaic and Fremont figures are thought to be visions the shamans saw while in a trance.

The Ute figures are the latest and show horses, which were gained from Spanish settlement during the 17th century. Noble

Sego Canyon is near a once flourishing little town of *Thompson*. Now it's still charming, but not flourishing.

The *cafe* was featured on the movie Thelma and Louise. There is also a *historic school*, built in 1907.

How to get to Sego Canyon, Utah:

Sego Canyon is north of Thompson, Utah, off of I-70. Drive through Thompson and continue on 4 miles to the parking area.

Southeastern Utah

Natural Bridges National Monument

Capitol Reef

Capitol Reef

Magnificent **Capitol Reef National Monument** has it all, including spectacular scenery, an old homestead cabin, and petroglyphs.

My favorite feature of Capitol Reef is the **Historic Pioneer Register**. This is where many early pioneers carved their names and dates into the rock. It is a permanent record of history, chiseled for all to see. It's a nice, easy stroll down a beautiful canyon, with names etched everywhere you look.

An amazing section of the register is six names, carved in 1911, way up on the rock. These pioneers must have repelled down the cliff face to carve the names.

There are also **petroglyphs** at Capitol Reef. They were chiseled by the Fremont culture in 300-1300 CE.

The **Behunin Cabin** is also within the grounds of the monument. It was built in 1882 by Elijah Behunin.

The cabin contains only one room and yet the entire family including Elijah, his wife, and 13 children lived in it.

Another beautiful historic building is the **one-room schoolhouse** built in 1896.

There are historical photos of some of the classes that went there. NPS

How to get to Capitol Reef, Utah:

Capitol Reef National Monument is 218 miles south of Salt Lake City. Take I-15 south, then take exit 188 for Hwy 50 and drive .7 miles. Turn right onto Hwy. 50 east and continue 24.4 miles. Turn right on to Hwy 260 and drive 4.2 miles. Turn right onto Hwy. 24 and continue 2.8 miles. Stay on Hwy 24 and drive 71.3 miles to the Capitol Reef Visitor Center.

Natural Bridges
National
Monument

Natural Bridges National Monument

T he ***Natural Bridges National Monument*** has 3 bridges, which were created by water flowing underneath them. They were discovered in 1883 by a prospector looking for gold. The spectacular bridges were published in National Geographic in 1904. You can drive a 9-mile scenic loop to see all of the bridges and other features of the monument.

The ***Sipapu bridge*** is the second largest natural bridge in the world; in Hopi, Sipapu is a gateway to the spirit world.

The ***Kachina bridge*** is the youngest of the three bridges; we know this by the thickness of its span.

Owachomo bridge, which is the Hopi word for rock mound.

The ruin at Natural Bridges National Monument known as the **Horsecollar Ruin**, so named because of the odd shaped windows in the granary building.

It was built around 1050 AD and abandoned about 700 years ago. People began living in the area 9000 years ago. NPS

How to get to Natural Bridges National Monument, Utah:

Natural Bridges National Monument is off Hwy 95, 42 miles west of Blanding, Utah

Edge of the Cedars

Edge of the Cedars

T he ***Edge of the Cedars Site*** contains ***Ancestral Puebloan ruins*** along with an excellent ***museum*** with a large sample of artifacts, including archaic spear throwers, stone tools, ornaments, and textiles, all beautifully presented.

The museum also contains the largest collection of Ancestral Puebloan pottery in the Four Corners area.

One of my favorite artifacts is a group of projectile points attached to a yucca string, all ready to go traveling with an ancient hunter.

Some of the more unusual items in the museum include a sash of macaw feathers, dating from around 1150 AD, discovered in a cave, and a copper bell which was traded from Mexico.

When you exit the museum, there is a trail that leads to a restored kiva, which you can enter using a ladder. There are also the ruins of a two story building, and kivas built between 1109 and 1117 AD. [Noble]

How to get to Edge of the Cedars, Utah:

Edge of the Cedars State Park is in southeastern Utah near Blanding, off Hwy 163.

A word about kivas:

The word *"kiva"* means cellar or underground house, and it was a special place of ceremony. Kivas were used primarily by men, but women and children could enter them for certain ceremonies and at certain times.

When an area was abandoned, kivas were often ritually closed by being filled in and sealed, and the roofs were burned.

Butler Wash

Butler Wash

T he ***Butler Wash Ruins*** were built over 700 years ago by Ancestral Puebloan people, formerly known as Anasazi.

The **cliff dwellings** are wonderful. They contain four **kivas** (ceremonial centers) including a square-shaped one, representing Mesa Verde culture.

Ancient residents accessed the cliff dwellings using a hand and toe-hold trail carved into the rock. The trail is still visible, but very worn down in some areas.

The residents benefitted from a southern exposure, which kept the dwellings warm in the winter, and cool in the summer. [Noble]

How to get to Butler Wash, Utah:

The Butler Wash ruins are 14 miles west of Blanding, Utah along Hwy 95.

Newspaper Rock

Newspaper Rock

Newspaper Rock is a fabulous rock art site. There are so many images on each boulder, it's incredible to see. It is one of the most densely packed petroglyph panels in the southwest.

The site contains multiple cultures including Archaic, Fremont, Ancestral Puebloan, Ute, Navajo, and Basketmaker, plus some Spanish and early pioneer etchings, including horses and a wagon wheel.

The Archaic images are over 2000 years old, and the Fremont images are dated between 500 and 1300 AD. The images of horses are after the Pueblo revolt of 1680, when horses were traded in the valley. [Noble]

How to get to Newspaper Rock, Utah:

Newspaper Rock is south of Moab, on the north side of Hwy 211, 13 miles west of the intersection with Hwy 191.

A word about rock art:

There are several cultural periods of rock art, including:

- *Archaic* 5000 BCE to 300 CE

- *Basketmaker* 1000 BCE to 750 CE (oldest Ancestral Puebloan)

- *Fremont* 500 CE to 1400 CE (Utah and Colorado)

- *Ancestral Puebloan* 200 CE to 1600 CE (N. Arizona and NW New Mexico)

- *Hohokam* 300 CE to 1400 CE (S. Arizona)

- *Mogollon* 500 CE to 1250 CE (SE Arizona and SW New Mexico)

- *Historic* begins 1540 CE after European contact

A moment in time:

In 1680, the ***Pueblo Indian Revolt*** began. It was a well-planned and well-executed rebellion against the harsh rule of Spain. Since the colonization in 1598, the once peaceful Pueblo Indians were treated with severe punishments including whipping, slavery, and hard labor, dismemberment of their hands or feet, and hanging.

The Pueblo Indians were forced to destroy objects sacred to them and fill in their ceremonial centers, the kivas, all in an effort to stamp out their religion in favor of Christianity.

Finally after so many decades, they rose up against their Spanish captors, led by a medicine man, named Pope, from the San Juan Pueblo. He led the revolt against the Spanish, on August 10, 1680.

Eleven days later, the Spaniards retreated, after the deaths of 400 people, including 21 priests. The Pueblos remained free for twelve years, until 1692, when New Mexico again came under Spanish rule with Governor Pedro de Vargas.

Mule Canyon

Mule Canyon Ruins

The **Mule Canyon Ruins** main occupation was from 1000 AD to 1150 AD by the Ancestral Puebloan people. (Formerly Anasazi)

The ruins include what was once a 12 room pueblo, kiva, and tower. The tower has a line-of-sight to other towers a mile away, which suggests it may have been used for signaling purposes or that it had an astronomical use.

Mule Canyon also has a wonderful **dinosaur site**, with a gorgeous, easy hike full of dinosaur fossils you can see, still embedded in the rock.

There are bones of large, plant-eating sauropods, weighing up to 20 tons, and of meat-eating allosaurus, which grew up to 30 feet long. [Noble]

I camped here too, in a pretty campground run by the BLM. There are only 10 spots, so hurry. I woke up to a beautiful pronghorn antelope. Life is good in Utah.

How to get to Mule Canyon, Utah:

Mule Canyon is along Hwy 95, 16 miles east of spectacular Natural Bridges National Monument.

Ghost Story:

Recapture Creek, located between Bluff and Blanding, Utah, is the site of lost gold, found by the Spaniards sometime around 1760. The gold was mined by Indians which the Spaniards had enslaved.

After the gold was mined, the Spaniards set the Indians free, who promptly turned on the Spaniards and killed them all, including their poor burros.

The Indians buried the dead Spaniards, the burros, and all of the gold, including several gold bars. Local legend says there is a curse on the gold, bringing death to whomever may find it. John C. Fremont claimed to have found the burro skeletons sometime between 1842 and 1844.

In fact, gold has been found by several individuals including a cowboy in 1905, who found a gold bar with a cross stamped on it. He had a partner, and together the two of them went looking for more gold. The partner was killed during a card game, and the cowboy was later killed by outlaws.

Two amateur archaeologists also found gold in 1964, but later disappeared. Then, in 1994, a research group found gold bars with the date 1761 stamped on them. Dunning

Hovenweep
National
Monument

Hovenweep National Monument

*H**ovenweep National Monument* is one of my favorite archaeological sites because of the sheer size and majesty of the ruins. The hike is easy, around the perimeter of a huge canyon. The view is spectacular everywhere you look.

Tall, fortress-like buildings stand along various points of the canyon. The buildings were constructed from 1230 to 1275 CE, about the same time as Mesa Verde. NPS

No one has lived at Hovenweep for over 700 years. Population growth, deforestation, loss of resources and drought may have caused the people to abandon Hovenweep. In fact, the word Hovenweep means deserted valley in Ute/Paiute.
Noble

As you walk along, you will see the *Eroded Boulder House*, a structure which uses a large boulder for the roof. The *Stronghold House*, was built like a fortress and people gained access by climbing hand and foot holds or a wooden ladder.

At *Hovenweep Castle*, growth rings on a tree show a date of 1277 CE making it one of the later buildings built here.

How to get to Hovenweep National Monument, Utah:

Hovenweep extends from Utah through Colorado. From Hwy 191 in Utah, take Hwy 262 for 8 miles, then turn left on Hwy 401 for 16 miles, then left at the sign for Hovenweep.

As you drive along, look out for beautiful wild horses, like this mama and her baby.

A word about what happened:

What happened to these ancient cultures which caused them to abandon their monumental buildings:?

- The Mimbres culture disappeared around 1130 AD

- Chaco Canyon, North Black Mesa, and Ancestral Puebloan all disappeared middle to late 1100's

- Mesa Verde and Kayenta cultures disappeared around 1300 AD

- Mogollon culture disappeared around 1400 AD

- Hohokam disappeared late into the 1400's

It was probably a combination of factors that caused the residents to abandon their homes. One of the main causes was a major multi-year drought beginning around 1130 AD. Cultures were impacted differently by this, depending on whether they lived in an area with more or less rainfall. Those that lived at higher elevations with more rainfall tended to cope with the drought better.

Cultures with larger populations like Chaco Canyon, exhausted their food supply more quickly, resulting in conflict over food, land, and other resources. There is some evidence of cannibalism, because human muscle protein has been found in the dried fecal material of ancient humans. Major conflict was inevitable, and it is widely believed that ancient survivors were absorbed into other cultures like the Zuni. Diamond

Southwestern Utah

Grafton

Fremont Indian State Park

Fremont Indian State Park

T he **Fremont Indian State Park** is wonderful. The scenery
is spectacular, with brilliant rust colored stone enhanced by
green trees everywhere.

There are many panels of
petroglyphs throughout the park
and scattered along hiking trails.

The **Visitor's Center** has an
excellent selection of artifacts,
including gaming pieces, found
during excavations in the park.
You can also get a map in the
Visitor's Center of the various
hiking trails, petroglyphs, and
facilities in the park.

The Fremont Culture were
named for the Fremont River
which runs close to many
Fremont Sites. The river in turn,
was named for John C. Fremont,
the famous explorer.

The Fremont Culture inhabited this area for 1000 years, starting from about 300 AD and lasting until about 1300 AD. ^{Noble}

There are several excellent hiking trails in the park, including the *Parade of Rock Art*, *Court of Ceremonies*, *Cave of 100 Hands*, and the *Arch of Art*.

In the park, there is a site, known as the *Belknap Station*, which was once an early Forest Service Ranger Station, built sometime between 1910 and 1915. Early ranger stations were built near meadows and streams to feed the ranger's horses. They were single-room cabins built within a day's horseback ride from each other.

Rangers would stay in the cabins as they patrolled their routes. As accessibility improved with roads, the cabins turned into family dwellings where the rangers could stay for months with their families. Fremont Indian State Park

How to get to Fremont Indian State Park and Belknap Station, Utah:

Fremont Indian State Park is in central Utah, near Sevier. Take exit 17 off I-70 and follow the signs to the park entrance.

Profiles in history:

Gifford Pinchot was born in 1865 and graduated from Yale in 1889. He served as the first head of the United States Forest Service when it was established in 1905, and he has been called the "father of the forest service." He became friends with President Theodore Roosevelt and shared his love of the land and the importance of preserving it through conservation. Pinchot continued to advocate for conservation until his death in 1946.

Parowan Gap
Petroglyphs

Parowan Gap

The ***Parowan Gap Petroglyphs*** are near Parowan, Utah, and they are fantastic. There are over 90 panels with 1500 figures. It is believed some are almost 5000 years old. The Parowan Gap area has been inhabited for at least the last 12,000 years.

Some of the petroglyphs were incised by Archaic people, but most were the work of the Fremont culture from about 300 AD.

Petroglyph images include clan symbols, animals, human figures, directional references, and the spiral, which is the Hopi migration symbol.

There are also geometric forms, one of the most curious of which is the Zipper Glyph. Its meaning is a mystery, however, some Hopi believe it to be a map recording the travels of a group of people. Others believe it is part of a solar and lunar calendar system. Noble

Many early explorers and homesteaders made their way through Parowan Gap, leaving small messages behind. In 1776, the Dominguez-Escalante Spanish explorers came into the Parowan Gap attempting to find a route from New Mexico to Monterey, California.

How to get to Parowan Gap, Utah:

Parowan Gap is near the town of Parowan, which is north of Cedar City. Drive west off of Main Street in Parowan, and continue on 400 North for 10.5 miles.

A word about the Dominguez Escalante Expedition:

Two Franciscan priests named Francisco Atanasio Dominguez, who was 36 years old, and 26 year-old Silvestre Velez de Escalante, planned to leave Santa Fe on July 4, 1776, the same day as the signing of the Declaration of Independence.

Their goal was to find a route over land from Santa Fe, New Mexico to their mission in Monterey, California. They eventually left Santa Fe on July 29th, traveling over two thousand miles over New Mexico, Colorado, Arizona, and Utah. They never reached Monterey or the Pacific Coast. Crutchfield

Cedar City

Frontier Homestead State Park

The settlement of **Cedar City** began in 1850, when Mormon Leader Brigham Young asked for volunteers to help mine iron ore, a precious commodity for growing towns. The ironworks established in Cedar City only lasted about 8 years, when it was closed in 1858.

Frontier Homestead State Park has an excellent museum and several historic buildings moved there from surrounding areas.

One very special building is known as the ***"teacherage"*** a combination classroom on the ground floor, and a cozy teacher's lodgings on the upper floor.

Inside the museum, there is a fascinating collection of old wagons and vehicles, including an early version of a snowmobile from 1941..

Early Snowmobile

Conquistador Armor

My favorite artifact in the museum is a set of conquistador armor found in the area. It's possible the armor came from two Franciscan priests named Atanasio Dominguez and Silvestre Velez de Escalante, who came through this area of Utah in 1776. They were trying to find a route over land from Santa Fe, New Mexico to their mission in Monterey, California. Utah State Parks

How to get to Cedar City:

Cedar City is 250 miles south of Salt Lake City on I-15.

A word about Mormon handcarts:

Not all of the Mormon settlers could afford a wagon to carry their belongings. In 1856, many used handcarts, which they would push or pull forward. The Mormon Handcart was a 60 pound contraption with two wheels. It was 7 feet long including the handles.

The Mormon settlers traveled through Illinois, Iowa, Nebraska, and Wyoming, before finally reaching Utah. The handcart cargo area was 3 feet wide, 4 feet long, and 8 inches deep. Each adult was allowed 17 pounds of personal items, and each child was allowed 10 pounds. The total weight of a handcart was about 130 pounds, and the handcarts were pushed or pulled the entire 1300 miles to Utah.

Each handcart company was given 2 wagons to carry provisions. During the years 1856 to 1860, 10 handcart companies formed, taking about 3% of the total Mormon settlers in their groups. At least 250 of these handcart pioneers died before reaching Utah.
Wagner

Grafton

Grafton

Grafton sits at the base of Zion National Park and is absolutely beautiful in a desolate kind of way. The town came into existence when Mormon pioneers, sent out by Brigham Young, began to grow cotton. The year was 1859. Cotton was heavily planted instead of food crops, so very soon the settlers were having trouble feeding their families.

The nearby Virgin River flooded in 1862, causing Grafton residents to move the town a mile upstream, where it sits today. Grafton's population fell from 28 families in 1862 down to 3 families by 1920. The townspeople left from time to time due to Indian attacks.

As you walk into Grafton, visit the wooden *barn and the home of John and Ellen Wood*, built in 1877, the pretty *adobe schoolhouse*, built in 1886, and the *Alonzo and Nancy Russell home*, built in 1862. Also take note of the hand-hewn wooden *cabin of Louisa Maria Foster Russell*, built in1879.

Don't miss the *Grafton Cemetery*, containing the graves of between 74 and 84 people, including settlers, and Paiute Indians, who helped the settlers. Some of the settlers were killed by Indian raiders, and some died from diphtheria, scarlet fever, or murder by Indians. Two girls,

ages 13 and 14 died in a "swing accident." ^{Varney}

How to get to Grafton, Utah:

Grafton is 8 miles south of Zion National Park, near the town of Rockville.

Fun fact:

Grafton became the setting for some scenes from the movie Butch Cassidy and the Sundance Kid.

Favorite Places to Camp

S *impson Springs Campground* is a perfect home base to
visit the Simpson Springs Pony Express Station and Onaqui
Wild Horse Management Area. The surroundings are spectacular,
and the campground has 20 sites which cost $15/night. There are
vault toilets and seasonal water.

—••⊖✦⊖••—

Dinosaur National Monument has the gorgeous ***Green River Campground***, a wonderful place to camp, right next to the Green River. There are 80 sites, some of which you can reserve through ***www.recreation.gov*** and others are available on a first come, first served basis. There are flush toilets, fire pits, but no showers.

Mule Canyon Campground is a small campground maintained by the BLM. There are only a handful of spots, and they fill up in a hurry. The place is rustic, remote, and the perfect place to enjoy the Mule Canyon ruins and dinosaur site at your leisure. There are nice little platforms from which to see the dinosaur tracks. Mule Canyon has vault toilets, but no other facilities, and the camping is FREE.

—••⊖✦⊖••—

Fremont Indian State Park Campground has 44 sites, 7 of which have full hook-ups. Fees range from $20 for a primitive site, to $35 for a full hook-up site. There are also 2 cabins, and various other sites. Campsites can be reserved through ***reserveamerica.com***, or on the Fremont Indian State Park Campground website.

Random Thoughts
What History Means to Me

F irst, let me start by sharing with you my opinion of what history isn't. History is not a collection of random dates, names, and places for you to memorize. History is not a dry and uninteresting class you have to pass to graduate.

I believe history is a tangible thing. You can actually *feel* history in the places you go, and the sights you see. I remember walking up to the Acropolis in Athens. I looked down at the well-worn marble steps and wondered about how many ancient philosophers had climbed these very steps, thousands of years ago.

You don't have to go far away to experience the *feeling* of history. If you are lucky enough to live in an old house, you may experience history in your own surroundings. You might say to yourself, *"If only these walls could talk."*

During my travels across the United States, I *felt* history in many, many places. If you travel across the country like I did, you will *feel* the wonderful history of our beautiful country for yourself, and you will never be the same. You will discover what it means to be an American.

———❖———

Why I did it and why you can too:

I decided to travel across the country by car because I wanted to rediscover America. When I first set out to explore the history of our country, I wanted to find out why America is the greatest country on earth, and what it means to be an American.

The politics of these United States was frightening at the time. Our country was polarized, almost beyond repair. Whether it was Democrats or Republicans, Conservatives, or Liberals, everyone was fighting.

I wanted to rediscover the joy of being an American. I wanted to rediscover our rich history, our unique and wonderful people, our tapestry of multicultural heritage, and our rich natural resources. I thought a road trip by car across eleven western states was a good place to start.

I have a degree in Archaeology, and a passion for all things archaeological. I love history, with a side love of paleontology. It is these three passions that I set my trip agenda around. I set out to discover the archaeological sites, history, and paleontological world of our country.

As I travel and write my books, I get asked all the time, especially by women, "What is it like to travel by yourself? Aren't you scared?" The truth is, I believe everyone should do what I did. It's a wonderful way to discover our country, and to rediscover yourself. The truth is, I'm scared not to travel. Traveling allows you to get to know yourself, in ways not possible when sitting on the couch watching TV.

We tend to spend a lot of our lives tuning out the world and our place within it. When you travel, you are quite literally forced to deal with your own thoughts, emotions, and feelings. You can discover yourself while traveling. You can come to understand what makes you who you are, and how you can perhaps become a better person. Above all, traveling gives you mental clarity to figure out how to live with intent. It's a way to guide your life, not just wait for things to happen.

Travel Tips & Stuff
What You Need to Know

How to get started:

P lanning your trip should be one of the most exciting things about it. You want to be spontaneous, but it is also very wise to plan your route, so you can take full advantage of all the time and miles you will invest.

First, decide your passions. If you love airplanes, trains, or old vehicles, plan your trip around that. If you love gardens or architecture, seek that out as the focus of your trip.

Next, read and research areas of the country that will let you enjoy what you are interested in.

- Make a list by state and city or town, of what you want to see.

- Take your handy road atlas and locate the areas on the pages.

- Make a tentative route plan, so you have an idea of where you are going.

Travel tip: Avoid trying to plan your trip down to a schedule of days, hours, or minutes. On a road trip, it will be virtually impossible to know where you will be on any given day. If you adhere to a schedule, you are more likely to stress out, and less likely to actually enjoy yourself, which is the whole point.

What you need:

You need to bring along a sense of adventure and a curious mind. You need to ditch the idea of always being on a schedule, and live a little more spontaneously to thoroughly enjoy yourself. Things will happen as you travel, both good things and bad things, and you need to prepare your mind and your soul for day-to-day changes.

So much of our lives are planned out. Between growing up, going to school, finding a career, marriage, kids, or whatever, people have lost much of the ability to be spontaneous. But you must take spontaneity on the trip with you, because you may make detours along the way to see something really spectacular.

So, for the practical stuff you need:

A great vehicle-I have a Honda CRV which is fabulous. It's old, a 2004, fully paid for, and will go anywhere. I see humongous RVs on the road, towing a car behind, and all I can think of is, they can't go just anywhere. They are too big. Bad gas mileage, cumbersome to drive, slow, and not agile like my CRV. So, I encourage you, if you want to go car camping and be able to go on remote dirt roads, get an agile vehicle, and Hondas are great.

Travel tip: Don't be afraid to do some modifications to your vehicle. I took one of my back seats out. (after watching a YouTube video) I threw in a twin mattress, a bit of drapery, and some netting. I also put some of those little portable light switches on the inside. I jettisoned anything I hadn't used up to that point. Don't be afraid to get rid of unnecessary stuff.

An awesome camera that you know inside and out. I use a Nikon and it takes wonderful pictures. Don't skimp on a camera, and don't think a cellphone camera is all you need, because you want the best for your beautiful photos.

A hot plate warmer-this little item was indispensable. You need a converter for it so you can plug it in to the cigarette lighter. Place your food inside it, carton and all, and then plug it in. 30 minutes for thawed food, about an hour and a half for frozen food. Boom! You have a hot meal by the time you stop for the night!

Window shades-the best ones are magnetic so you just place them against your windows and they cling to them, obscuring the view inside your car.

Portable cooler with wheels-another indispensable item that works great and is easy to move around. I use those nifty blue frozen blocks in mine.

Portable air compressor-this little gem plugs into your cigarette lighter and will inflate your tires if you have a flat. Fortunately, I haven't had to use this yet.

Portable battery charger and power bank-mine comes with battery cables and the power bank, yet once inside the case, it is small enough to put in your glove compartment. This little item, unfortunately, I have had to use, and it saved me.

Portable generator-mine came with a small solar panel, so it can be charged with solar or electricity. It has a decent battery life and also doubles as a light for night-time.

All season clothing-you never know what different states will bring for weather, so take hot weather and cold weather clothes, and a fair amount of shoes appropriate for hiking, or walking, sandals, and slippers, which are nice at night. Also take along a pair of cheap rubber flip-flops to wear in the public showers you might go into.

Your own pillows-I like my own pillows, so I don't wake up with neck cramps, especially after sleeping in the car.

Sleeping bag and cozy blankets-you want to stay warm and layering is everything.

Warm hat, warm socks, and fuzzy jammies to keep you warm for cold nights sleeping in the car.

A great road atlas, and great guidebooks-get one that's easy to read, with great pictures. For a road atlas, just get one that is easy to read.

A word about photography:

Along with a great camera, you need to have a great eye. This is easier than it sounds once you have worked with your camera and are comfortable taking pictures with it. I am not a professional photographer, but I like my pictures and other people do too.

These are my tips for taking great pictures:

- Experiment with taking both horizontal and vertical shots.

- Don't always put the subject of the photo in the middle of the photograph.

- This one is important: pay attention to the foreground, and if possible, have something, a plant or whatever, in the foreground to help give the photo dimension and depth.

- This one is important too: turn around often to see the view you just came from. I do this quite often and some of my best pictures have resulted from when I turned around and took the shot.

You can also take a mental photo. Place an image in your mind that you can call upon later. Use all of your senses to see, hear, smell, and maybe even to taste, what is around you. You have the means to fully experience your surroundings, and that is very important to a traveler. When you take a mental photo, be sure to jot down quick little details about what you saw, heard, smelled, or tasted, so you can jog your memory later.

And last, but not least...don't be posing in front of everything, everywhere, to show that you actually went somewhere. Most people want to see themselves in your photo and be mentally transported there, but they can't if you are there already.

—◦✦◦—

To camp or not to camp:

Car camping is great. I prefer it to sleeping on the cold, hard ground in a tent. I can lock the doors, put my window shades up and be cozy for the night.

That being said, for me there were some do's and don'ts about camp sites. Some people camp in a Walmart parking lot and feel safe. I do not. I believe that if you are in a busy area, you're more likely to be confronted by a nut job who may bother you. Nothing against Walmart.

Same goes for casino parking lots. Many people believe that if they are in a public place, there is less chance of someone bothering them. I don't share this belief. I believe you are safer parked out in the middle of nowhere in the dark. That same nut job who can find you in a parking lot is not about to go driving around on dirt roads to see if anyone is parked there. At least that's my belief. You may not share it, and that's fine. Park and camp wherever you feel safe.

I don't go for rest areas either because they have a track record of incidents happening to people in rest areas, especially women travelers.

So, where do I camp? In state or national campgrounds, wildlife sanctuaries, or off on a dirt road somewhere, usually out in the middle of nowhere.

There are definitely times when I stay in a motel. I use Hotels.com because I like their stay 10 nights, get 1 night free deal. So, I book a hotel or motel if:

- The weather is too hot or too cold, or too rainy

- I am in a city and plan to stay awhile

- I'm tired of camping, need a shower, or my body hurts

- I need to do laundry

A word about safety:

When you are a woman traveling alone, it's critical to keep a low profile. Don't tell people you are traveling alone, where you are staying, or any other personal information.

I don't go to bars or get drunk. I'm not preaching but you are on your own, in a city or town you've never been to, and you don't know anyone, so it's not the time to lose control of what you are doing. When you are in control, you are better able to decide which people you want to get to know better.

Travel tip: If you feel vulnerable traveling alone, that's OK. Vulnerability is part of passion, and traveling is a passionate thing to do. You can put one of those family stickers on your vehicle to indicate to others that you are not traveling alone, which can help you feel more secure.

Maintain your connections:

When you are traveling alone, there is a definite sense of disconnection. It feels almost like you are the only one in the world, traveling through space and time. That's why it's critical to keep your connections to loved ones active.

Be on Facebook while you are traveling. You may not have internet a lot of the time, or the internet will be poor. Consider paying to have your phone be a hotspot. It's a little bit of money per month, but it's worth it and has saved me from being without internet. I love the convenience of it, and you will too.

Plan your journey around visiting family members or friends you haven't seen for a long time, or people that are good friends. When you see people you know, it will ground you, so you can continue traveling.

Check in by phone with loved ones. They worry about you, and it's good for both of you to stay connected no matter where you are.

Consider traveling with a pet. I started my trip with my beloved 14-year-old sheltie named Sadie. She didn't make it to the end of the trip. I lost her to bladder cancer about four months in. My Sadie was special, and I will never forget my first traveling buddy.

It took me a solid year to decide on getting another dog. I poured over profiles of rescue dogs, looking for a little buddy I could take care of. Best Friends Animal Society in Kanab, Utah, had my perfect match. I now have Rosie, an 8 year-old sheltie that looks just like Sadie and has many of the same mannerisms. Life is good again.

I highly recommend Best Friends Animal Society if you are looking for a pet. They have 3000 acres and house up to 1600 animals at one time including dogs, cats, horses, pigs, and just about everything else. The dedicated people at Best Friends are wonderful both to you, and your potential pet.

Travel tip: One of the easiest and best ways I stay connected while traveling is to offer to take a photo for someone I don't know. Many couples, families, or singles would love to have more pictures of themselves traveling. It's an easy and quick way to have a connection with a fellow traveler, and it's good manners too.

Practical matters:

You need to have an address to send your mail to. Keep in touch with whomever is nice enough to do this for you.

You will also need to come back occasionally to register your car, vote, go to doctor visits, and take care of any other business. You can't leave it all behind, as tempting as that may be.

Bad things that happened:

Remember when I said you need to take spontaneity with you on your trip? Well, there were many times when I used my spontaneity skillset.

The government shutdown happened smack dab in the middle of my travels. That meant that all of the National Monuments were closed. I did a lot of driving and circling around.

I also did a lot of circling around trying to avoid natural disasters. I traveled through Paradise, California shortly before a massive fire happened there. I tried to travel through the area again but was pushed out by massive flooding. My latest event was camping in Canyonville, Oregon and waking up to flames creeping down the hillside. That was day one of the Canyonville fire.

Besides being driven out by natural disasters, sometimes I was driven out by rude people. Many times it was centered around my furry traveling companion. I believe there are really only two types of people, those who love animals and those who don't. When people see me walking my beautiful, sweet, elderly dog, they either come up and pet her, or they say something harsh.

One incident was a woman, a total stranger, who came up to me smiling down at Sadie and asked how old she was. I replied, "She is 13 and a half years old." The woman replied very curtly "She needs to be put down." Sadie was walking around, alert, and happy, and yet this woman wanted me to end her life because she was old.

Speaking of animals, several times I came very close to driving into an animal on the road. I can't stress enough how many times this will happen to you, and all I can say is, be alert at all times while you are driving. When you travel a lot of miles, you will get tired, so stop and smell the roses, and try not to drive at night.

Good things that happened:

One of the sheer joys of taking a road trip is the unpredictability of it. You never know what you will see. I am originally from Oregon, and bears are not a common sight. So, while driving high up in the Blue Mountains, I looked over and saw a bear! So exciting! He didn't stay for long, kind of shy, but so cute. I love animals, so to see the rich and wonderful amount of wildlife in our country gladdened my heart.

I met many great people on my trip, from all walks of life. They were a walking, talking advertisement for our beautiful country. I smiled at them, and they smiled back. We are all Americans, and we are all part of the human race. When you meet people across the country, you realize just how important it is to get to know your fellow citizens, and learn more about how they view the world and our country.

I have to give a special shout-out to the many dedicated people, often volunteers, who staff our state and national parks and monuments. They work tirelessly to ensure the health of our natural resources, and help travelers enjoy their visit. The same is true of the many people who staff the museums in small towns and large cities. They enjoy history, like I do, and it shows in their smiles.

Along with wonderful people, I have seen an America that is spectacularly beautiful, with open prairies, majestic mountains, and crystal clear rivers. I have seen a small fraction of the history of our country. I have seen the memorials to the brave people who shaped our country. I have fallen in love with America in a way that was not possible sitting in my living room. People ask me, "would I do it again?" The answer comes easily, "Yes, in a heartbeat."

Bibliography and Further Reading

*A*ntelope Island State Park, Utah State Parks, 0AD.

Balfour, Amy C. *Southwest USA's Best Trips: 32 Amazing Road Trips*. Lonely Planet, 2014.

Bandelier National Monument Main Loop Trail Guide, Western National Parks Association, 0AD.

The Buckhorn Wash Pictograph Panel, Bureau of Land Management, 0AD.

Chino, Conroy. *Petroglyphs of the Southwest: a Puebloan Perspective*. Western National Parks Association, 2012.

Corbett, Christopher. *Orphans Preferred: the Twisted Truth and Lasting Legend of the Pony Express*. Broadway Books, 2004.

Crutchfield, James A. *It Happened in Colorado: Remarkable Events That Shaped History*. TwoDot, 2017.

Diamond, Jared M. *Collapse: How Societies Choose to Fail or Succeed*. Penguin Books, 2011.

Dunning, Linda. *Restless Spirits: Utah's Small Town Ghosts*. CFI, 2010.

Enss, Chris. *Tales behind the Tombstones*. Morris Pub., 2007.

Fielding Garr Ranch 1848-1981, Utah State Parks, 0AD.

Finch, etc. al.., Jackie. *Eyewitness Travel USA*. DK Publishing, 2017.

Fremont Indian State Park , Fremont Indian State Park , 0AD.

Frontier Homestead State Park, Utah State Parks, 2016.

Glassman, Steve. *It Happened on the Santa Fe Trail*. Twodot, 2008.

Hovenweep Little Ruin Trail Guide, National Park Service,

Hovenweep, National Park Service

Krause, Mariella. *Southwest USA's Best Trips: 32 Amazing Trips*. Lonely Planet, 2014.

Mayo, Matthew P. *Haunted Old West: Phantom Cowboys, Spirit-Filled Saloons, Mystical Mine Camps, and Spectral Indians*. Globe Pequot Press, 2012.

Mormon Ferry at the Upper Crossing of The North Platte, Fort Caspar Museum

Natural Bridges Visitor Guide, National Park Service, 0AD.

Navajo National Monument, National Park Service, 0AD.

Noble, David Grant. *Ancient Ruins and Rock Art of the Southwest: an Archaeological Guide*. Taylor Trade Publishing, 2015.

Noble, David Grant. *Ancient Ruins of the Southwest: an Archaeological Guide*. Northland Pub., 2000. .

Old Spanish Trail, Bureau of Land Management, 2012.

Park City Museum, Park City Museum, 0AD.

Parowan Gap Petroglyphs, National System of Public Lands

Rutter, Michael. *Bedside Book of Bad Girls: Outlaw Women of the American West*. Farcountry Press, 2008.

Smith, B. *Ghost Stories of the Rocky Mountains*. Lone Pine Pub., 1999.

Varney, Philip. *Ghost Towns of the Mountain West: Your Guide to the Hidden History and Old West Haunts of Colorado, Wyoming, Idaho, Montana, Utah, and Nevada*. MBI Pub. Co. and Voyageur Press, 2010.

Wagner, Tricia Martineau. *It Happened on the Oregon Trail: Remarkable Events That Shaped History*. GPP, 2014.

Weis, Norm. *Ghost Towns of the Northwest*. Caxton Printers, 2002.

Index

Referenced by Sections

About the Author

Julie Bettendorf is a world traveler with a degree in archaeology and a background in history. She has traveled extensively throughout Egypt, Central America, South America, Europe, and the United Kingdom, visiting archaeological and historical sites all along the way.

Currently, Julie is traveling around the US visiting ghost towns, ancient rock art sites, and archaeological wonders as part of research for her ongoing historical travel series entitled *Wandering Woman*. Wandering Woman is a set of state-by-state guides, full of photographs, historical anecdotes, and unique tips to help other women travel and explore solo across the US by car. Julie enjoys writing freelance blogs, traveling frequently with her two adult children, and hiking outdoors with her faithful dog companion Rosie.

Also By Julie Bettendorf

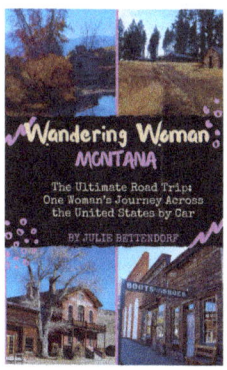

Wandering Woman: Utah is the second book in the Wandering Woman Travel Series. The first book ***Wandering Woman: Montana*** is available in ebook and paperback.

Julie has published two children's books in an ongoing, beautifully illustrated travel series entitled Anthony Ant Goes to France and Anthony Ant Goes to Egypt.

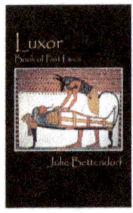

She has also published a work of historical fiction entitled Luxor: Book of Past Lives which has recently been released as an audiobook, read by renowned narrator Barry Shannon.

www.ingramcontent.com/pod-product-compliance
Lightning Source LLC
Chambersburg PA
CBHW070713130626
46553CB00005B/1969